ELEMENT 615

JOE BRUNDIDGE

Element 615

JOE BRUNDIDGE

First Edition 2017.

Edited by G. F. Harper.

Books may be purchased in quantity and/or special sales by contacting the publisher, Lit City Press: hello@litcitypress.com.

Published by Lit City Press (Lit City Publishing), Austin, Texas.

Cover and Interior Design by Lit City Press, Austin, Texas.

Cover Art, © 2017, Emily Clark | eclark.studio@gmail.com

Interior Art, © 2017, G. F. Harper | gfharper@litcitypress.com

---

Brundidge, Joe –

Element 615 : Poetry/American / General

ISBN-13: 978-0692856635 (Lit City Publishing)

ISBN-10: 0692856633

Library of Congress Cataloging Number:

Lit City Press (Lit City Publishing)

Austin, Texas.

Printed in the United States of America.

DEDICATION

To three of the greatest miracles I have ever known; my God given children -- Kreshon, Kiera, and Khari. I do it to prove you can do more; that you have the right to.

To my first best friend; my brother Bryan Brundidge. To my sister; nothing less than my heart, Vivian Brundidge. I cannot say how much I love you both; and I'll never be able to.

To my Joyce; my Ruby; thank you. To my aunt Joanie; my favorite Taurus; I love you. To my God-given father, Joe Capes Brundidge I; for teaching me how to be air as well as stone; for teaching me that love is synonymous with regardless; to do right, no matter who knows I did. To the greatest friend I have known: Franchesca Simon-Hughley; thank you Rabbit for always being right on time. I love you ace. To my God-given brother, The Bronx King, Edwin Maldonado Jr. – you are the reason I am a stronger thing. To my God-given sister, Rebekah Maldonado – thank you for knowing I was never less than what you know of me; and loving me as proof of this.

CONTENTS

ACKNOWLEDGMENTS

I would like to acknowledge the following people for their support and say thank you to Dominique Robinson, the Hungry Poet's Society: Tina Journey Johnson, Roshawna & CocoaFire & Reado, Forressa Harrison, Christopher Michael, Gabriel, Lord Byron, Solo, & Omega; to my Neo Soul Family: Herman Mason III; Thank you Baby Sha, Ebony Flake aka Naomi Tene Austin aka Zen Thug, Allen Trey Stepter III & Racquel & Rockie & Gilford-Stepter, Jarvis & Francesca Hughley, Edwin & Rebecca Maldonado, Brian & Jo Francis, Kimberly Taylor & Jai Milano, Brandy & Michelle Ayers, Chris, Jane, & H-Town Fritz, Ebony Stewart, Da'Shade Moonbeam, Valerie Bridgeman (I love you Mama V), Justin The Joyful & Mama Roue, Qi & Chaka, Kalia Glover, Evie Worsham, Craig Sullender, Ric Scow-Williams, Cleo Calobreves, Francois Pointeau, Erin Cornett, Lisa Onland, Chris Mattix; to Thom, The Poet Of The World, James Jacobs, Deborah Cano-Peques, Ernie Basaldua, and Mike Thompson.

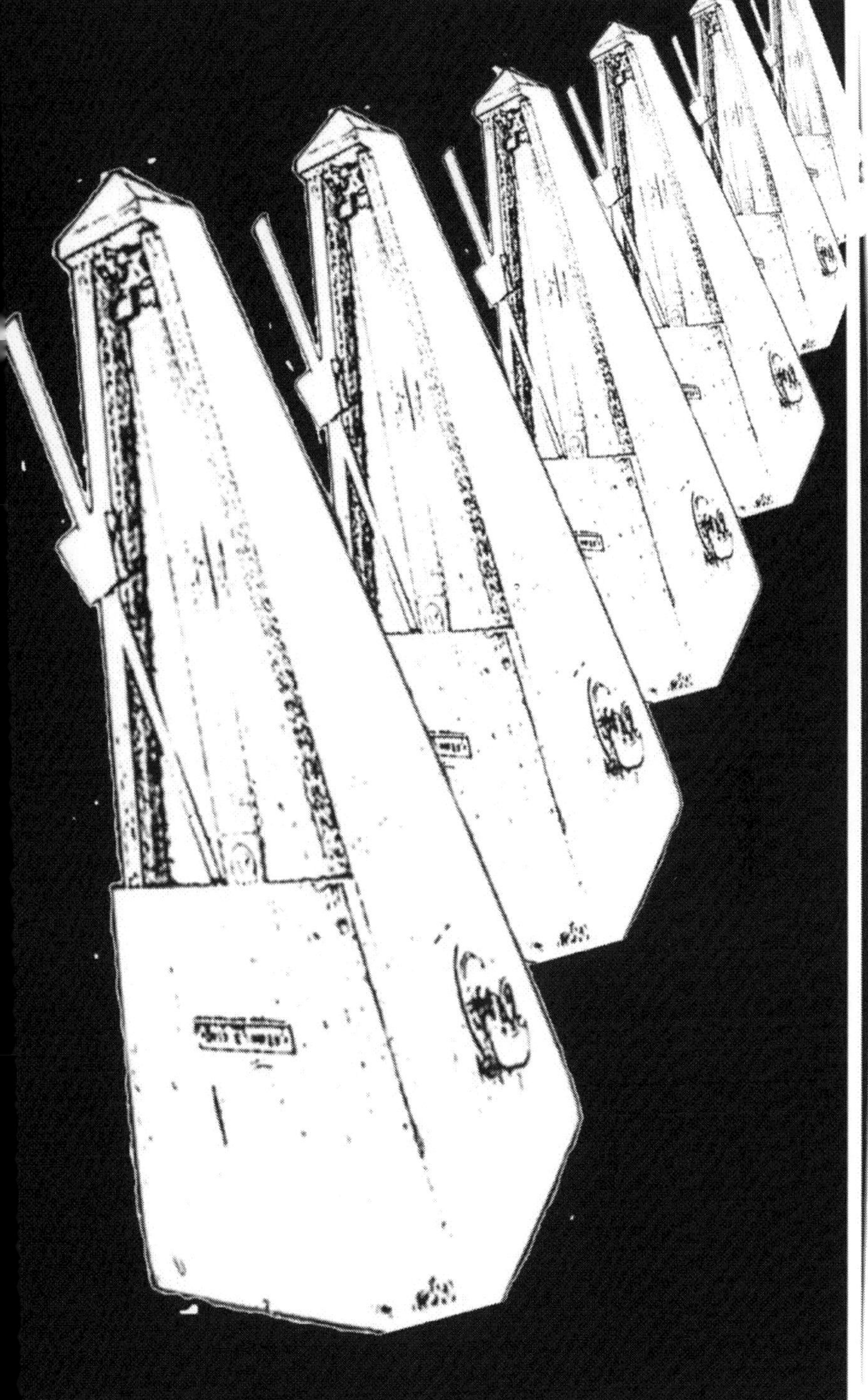

non-superfluous haiku

if you write like your
ink is blood then you will – no
doubt waste far less words

muted

say it's because you're busy
you'll lose track of time
miss the bus, or
you're on the bus, and

you'll miss your stop or
you're at work, and bills
take precedence
the timing isn't right

you don't have the right pen
there are books
to be read; your chakras
aren't aligned

the environment isn't right
you got allergies; congested
crowded in more ways
than one

maybe it’s too much on your mind
it's not something grown-ups do
and besides, it's already too late
in the evening; you have to get up

early to work, early to sleep
though you’ve never said it before
maybe you still feel guilty
having lost so much time

the last stretch
you gave into it
so you just lie; tell everyone
you've lost it

knowing full well
it’s right there; breathing
on the back of your neck; maybe
you're still in that room

you still remember
holding her hand
saying hello, as her eyes
said goodbye

maybe it's all too much
life like a room full of people
walk out the door at once
and you refuse

to acknowledge the insurrection
inside; telling folks you're fine
they can see the fissures
on your face

you've become
preoccupied with running and
you stopped caring about
where you were heading

or maybe, just maybe
you finally got hit
by so much you're
unincorporated now

pieces
of you spread
over the whole
of your existence

pieces
of you; but the show
must gone on
especially when

you're not on stage
life is not a stage
it's not a room full of people
staring at you

you prefer claustrophobia
to your fear of heights

maybe you're busy
trying to save the world
even though no one asked
this of you

maybe it's because
there's a lot of things

going on; maybe
no one will care

maybe you believe
the fire inside you
should asphyxiate
maybe

you hope to God
the anger inside stays
preoccupied
with eating at you

before it learns
a way out

say that you would rather
be master to your slave
than the captain
of your soul

Jupiter isn't aligned
with Atlantis; it's been years
since the doctor said
we need your permission

to terminate
and purgatory
has been every minute
after you said: yes

maybe, for whatever the reason
you prefer your light
in the valley
you've a lot going on

say you're afraid it's gone
you're afraid
it's still there
you are scared

of the big bad monster
that will come and make you
cleanse your soul
of all you won't let go

say that you have lost faith
in yourself; tell me what you
have to, but don't tell me
you've nothing to write.

efficient

I have pictures of memories
that fade a bit more
with every notice

they need to be
forgotten.
I no longer wonder

why a third of my
belongings is lost
with every move

I left the record
of my favorite smiles
in my last apartment

forgot to pack
those past embraces –
just the other day

I dropped off two bags
full of *wonder where you are*
keepsakes

thrift store tokens
because they don't fit
now

sold my *please*
come back for a pair of
I no longer care

and I have to tell you
they fit quite well
quite now

haiku 2

disenfranchised; you
ain't no Morlock; you ain't no

damn Eloy either

yep

I keep poking myself
on the head
tapping myself
on the head
with this pen
thinking
if I do it long enough
the poem will
shake loose

and
drop
down
through
one or both
of my nostrils
but only because
I don't open
my mouth
when I think

needless to say
I spent entirely
too much
damn time
on this poem
and as a
result

this is what
you got

apologies

education

I have been educated
in the way of things

I pray to a god
smaller than me

keep my head bowed
so that my hands don't pay
a price much like
I pay with my blood

sweat, and years
for little green pieces
of paper I can only call
receipts for my soul

some call them *sweat shops*
because even though
the tears eventually stop
perspiration never does

or maybe I'm wrong; maybe
more than sweat this is pride
washing out me; my family
lives with my ghost

a ghost who brings home
less than a paycheck and

even less than a person
I will put them to sleep

with stories of fantasy
like honor and humanity

none of my digits matter to you
but your clothes look nice

there is a picture of a forest
by a river in the break room
they are taunting us; they know
we will not leave, reminding us

of what we are too afraid
to fight for; they take pictures of us
smiling for their magazines
because that is all you need

to not give a damn. I say a prayer
that my children know the heaven
of dignity; that I am the stone
on the path to being more

than me; that they will never be
rolled back into oblivion, never
the target of those infected
with greed; I am no longer

a woman; I am the nameless
cattle with uniforms; a living

graveyard of smocks
no longer blind to the truth

I am beneath the shoes
I just made for you; not even
the lint in the jeans my fingers
stitched for you

I have been educated
in the way of things

haiku 3

dear today, please I
do not want you to die – we
have only just met

1

remind me
to leave you
a piece of me
in my will

should you not
want to wait that long
you have but to ask
you've had me

piecemeal
long before my bits
were anyone's
to begin with

if you don't mind
the bruises; you can have
the whole
damn thing

dust

I vacuumed
my lingering thoughts

accumulated, causing me
congestion

and once I could
actually think

the choice
to let it go

came
as easily

as the
decision

to end
this poem

right

here

(Period).

Asante

I did not beckon you
but I am glad you're here

didn't speak you
into existence; breathed
not one breath into you

but I'm no less grateful
to carry your name
in my lungs

haiku 4

eyelids heavy brain
soaked in fire pen itches
welcome to midnight

Sally

she walks a stretch
down the sidewalk
with cheap red heels
that began to talk

sometime ago –
a fading glow
shows itself

she walks with
a worn rhythm
no music to her; long
pink nightgown

once a dress
brown sun
beaten skin

she walks
crow's feet
beady eyes, worn
desensitized

from the lies
she was told
heart now empty

unable to hold
a hope or love

barely enough
for a smile, plenty
to help her say
I'll make it
worth your while

walking in a faded style
blocks turn to miles

unable to reconcile
with fate; the hand
she was dealt; see –
she no longer feels a thing
but when she did

she felt wrong for walking
along the streets

back then she had heart
she left it somewhere
sometime ago; sometime
between the sheets

her legs in the air
every part of her

to malignant despair
money changing hands
paid to be raped

all her days, dark
light never known

she lost sight
or never had it
never knew love
or the praise
of a queen

dress torn
rusty springs

of a bed; much like
where she lays
her head; she's a flower
she's fallen petals

a queen, lifeless
a queen, crying

that she is a woman
therefore she is love
that she is a woman
therefore she is wealth
but she is who she is

so her secret stays kept
by her heart, ham-fisted; because

it too lives in pain
with no one there

to share it with
no one for which
to explain, nothing

to listen to except
an elevated train

the drops from the faucet
falling down the drain
as she watches
each drop
into a dark hole

she wonders; which of those
drops is her soul?

joy

I knew of joy, because
I'd heard of it

I had heard it
heard it, alive

in a child's laugh; it was safe
in the space of a hug; people

embracing like God

this may be all the time
we have with each other

in my mother's eyes, it's there
my father's approving stare

because I had only seen it outside
myself, I assumed it was not mine

to own, but to give. I know joy

because I have fought for it
because I missed it, lost it –

in my loss of self; found it
discovered; living

in the corners
of you
your sanguine smile
safe
in the space
between us

I know joy

because
I know you

me and my brother haiku

I love you bro, please
kiss my niece for me.

Each time
I kiss her
I do

dear future lady of mine

I snore
it's a thing

I make up for it
in kind
custom made
hugs; saying
goofy things

to make you laugh
as you fall asleep

that right there
is a fair trade

yep

signed,
your dude

stronger things

tell yourself you can't

tell yourself not today
say you aren't able

you can't afford it
it's not the right time

you're not strong enough
no one else wants to

it's just you
it's too hot

it's too cold
you're tired

you don't feel right
it doesn't feel right

they'll say no
they'll say yes

you'll fail
and they'll all laugh

they'll all laugh

you'll die

you'll die
right there

so tell yourself any excuse
to avoid or evade

cite every drawback
cop out; tell yourself

anything to help you
believe you should do

nothing
and say it

loud enough
for me to hear you

I'll call you a liar
to your face; I'll grab you

pull you out

the mire the muck
mud of yourself

pity and douse you with water

of what I believe because

I believe you should end. I believe
you should die. I believe your life

should cease; so you can live the life
you held on back order; like the shoe

that actually fit; you're not allergic
to the light baby; you just don't want it

I don't get it because that
is all I see of you

when your arms aren't folded

acknowledge you have arms
quit complaining you don't have strength

because if that was the truth
you wouldn't hold on to things

like you do

you are not a prisoner
you are the warden

in a one person prison

what's worse
you're a workaholic

you wreak havoc
on your hopelessness

subtract it from the whole of you
believe less in your doubts

you cannot say that life is pointless
if you won't pick your head up

and look where it's pointing you
scream *I love you* in a crowd

loud enough for you to hear it
and revel in the nervous happiness

it's called glowing; you are everything
you wish you were; you just don't wish

to realize it; pass on the plate
of opinion unless

they can feed you and you not suffer
the indigestion of indecision

turn *why didn't I*
into *why didn't I do it sooner*

change *I don't know*
from question to statement

quit whining
unless

you're trying to make someone laugh
thereby making yourself a superhero

accept your own friend request
quit fighting with yourself unless

you're just sparring
for when you need to get it on

with anyone trying to knock you off

I'm not saying look for a fight
just don't run from it

pretending it's not there
doesn't mean it will go along

be the devil unto your demons
just because you created them

doesn't mean they get an easy ride
file a restraining order on yourself

restraint; and be the devil
unto your demons

just because you created them
doesn't mean they get a free ride

quit reading motivational posters

we both know
you
don't
listen
hell
you're probably not even paying attention
to this
poem

it's called
life

it happens

and yes baby
you
have to act

like you want it
but it is not yours. It is a path

it twists and it turns
you have to go

where it goes

and if you walk it
just right

you get to rest
while those not as far as you

ask you for directions

should you reach the end
there's only everything waiting

for you with the honor
of a memory; you

are so much more than misery
but it is not up to me to be you

just be grateful I know you
I am always standing with you

behind you; in front of you
above you; with all who love you
waiting for you

to erupt
from that thick husk

cut through the callous
of
your condition
call whatever comes
out your
character
to accept a truth
you won't hear

as you adhere to your cherished fears
that we are a
ma
zing

that we are made of both his
and each other's love

that we are both fearfully & wonderfully
made

that
we
are made of stronger things

dear future lover haiku

dear future lover
this thing -- that only we have
I indeed miss it

penance

tired
of being tired

God I
have so much
to do

so much
I need to do

I
don't ever want to sleep again

God
make me not
sleep
again

not until
that
very
last
time

dear hiccups

if you were a person
I'd steal
one of your
credit cards
find an automated DVD
rental kiosk

one I know you frequent
one I know you rent

as many movies
as possible
and burn them all

if you were a person
I'd replace
all of the sugar
in your home
with salt except
for the sugar
you've allotted
for your coffee
replacing it

with sleeping powder

basically
I'm trying to say
fuck you

task

there are lip magnets all over your body

land mines of joy

hidden well
on your person

it's my sworn duty
to locate and catalog each one

once I am done
stop

and start over
because I've forgotten

purposefully

damnation

I
demens
apparatus

I
pulchra
monstrum

there is
a hell
for me
called
why doesn't he get it
yet

I've been in a
barely lit
room
window
unlocked
door

smoking
the same cigarette
for the past
37 years

I have my ways
about me

if trying to make
your way to me
has given you
cause
to get away
from me

please know

if I never tell you
before I die
know
that the words
existed

they
were
in my
heart

I meant
every
one
of them

reside

houses are warm safe places
where all are welcome
to live as long as they please

replenishing its barren stores; yet
homes can be broken into
vandalized, robbed

of its stores; burned down
torn apart by wind and rain; and
all you can do is build

on what was there, in effigy
knowing full well what was
there will never be –

but if you were a castle
you wouldn't worry, for you
would be made of stone

you could fire your cannons
at anyone before they drew
close; surrounded by a moat

no one would dare cross –
you could have a drawbridge
with no one to lower it

you would have walls
with rooms unnumbered
so many rooms; you'd

never enter them all –
your own secret tunnels
to travel within, in secret

and to escape, should you
ever be overwhelmed
though this is not likely

but, if you were –
the mortar could be replaced
the walls built tall enough

too tall to scale
do not be a house

houses are effigies
to themselves

be a castle

montage

I wish
I had
a punching
bag

not to
train or
anything
like that

but just
to hit
when
I'm angry

and to
make me
feel like

I'm in a
montage

and while
I am in
my medley
of ferocity

I could
hit that bag

fist and fury
pointlessly
hard

hard
and fast
as if driven
by some
anger

some
poignant turmoil
visualizing
a fallen
loved one

imaginary foe
just bested me
in combat

prior to the montage
thus inspiring it

once I'm done
building
enough sweat

I can stop

the end

of my
mosaic
folly

having
effectively released
my faux-cinematic
rage. I really should

stop waiting
until 11:30 AM
to eat

shepherd

my mother would never let me keep the
daydreams
that followed me home

they would find me, running astray on their
own, and
I would play with them; roll around

and laugh with them in the middle of class
in the hall
and all the way home, where

my mother would be waiting; she would tell
me to send them away
as soon as I got to the doorstep

and though some were left behind, a few
would sneak in
I would feed them under the table

careful not to let her notice; though
my far off stares were
a dead giveaway; she knew her child

so she let a few stay, out of benevolence
and the fact
I'd have to learn to take care

of them eventually; see the problem with
dreamers – we make
horrible shepherds, often our flocks

get bigger than we can gather, we collect
more dreams
than we can tend to and

though we don't mean it, we let a few of
them die
my mother was a good teacher

haiku 6

I forgive my fears
for overprotecting me
I retire them

dear future lover

there will be
days when
I will
say *thank you*
and I will not
need a reason

there will be
nights when
I will hold you
a bit closer
you will ask
what's wrong?

and I will say
nothing
which will mean
I am grateful
there are
no more
nights

like tonight

Route 803

dear Mr. Pedestrian walking slow on the
crosswalk because you're texting –

clearly you DGAF

by the time you get your lame *do as you please*
looking ass across the street
it will be time for work tomorrow

matter of fact, I don't even think you work
over here; I think you just wake up every day

going to random crosswalks to upset the

natural order of things
that's what I think
matter of fact –

googling shit for no reason
you make me wish the bus had a horn

that rattled machine gun fire

moving slow like you in a hurry
to get back to yesterday
you make me wish

you could be catapulted across the street
or at least have God

put you somewhere

you make me want to get out of the bus
momentarily to beat you
with a whiffle ball bat

filled with rubber cement, until
you're safely across the street

hurry the hell up, please

sustenance

supping on
every sound you illicit
craving each crumb
of the delicious locution
you serve
in our conversations

my ears lick plate after plate
as we parlay; sucking
on your
sentences
to savor
your speech
and the sweet nectar of your
dialect
swallowing
your
luscious tone; my ears
begging my mouth
to ask
you for
bigger words; and now
my eyes numb
when they lose
sight of you

retinas quiver
on contact
silk to optic nerves

pupils dilating
as they learn to touch
your form; a symmetry
I dare not frame
with a texture; my extremities
could never fathom
more than simple
ocular ecstasy

everything
about you
embodies an aesthetic
with a singularly
flawless anatomy

I envy your unmentionables
embracing you
with every
encounter

Asante ii

you love that I
can make
the beast inside me
do such beautiful
things

I love
that it is
distracted

in the end, it's all about
any, which way
we can work it out

morning

this morning
the sun told me
the wind told him
it heard
I had not written a love poem
in quite some time

too busy running
to & from
simultaneously

swimming through regrets
sinking, the further I try
to kick the habit
if I am out of love
it's because
trying too hard to verb
lost me the noun
later that afternoon
the clouds told me
to quit feeling sorry for myself
to quit using them
as metaphors of self-pity
the rain reminded me
as it has before
if you are too willing
to be someone else's anything

it only breaks you down to nothing
yourself to blame
no one can love you
if you can't teach them how

by the time I saw the stars that night
they were already waiting
to add their two cents
singing in unison
there is much more to love
than waiting for someone
if you have not loved for the sake of love
how will it find you?
the moon just smiled; saying

I cannot have love if it is not something
I am not willing to be
I don't carry love in my arms
I do not deserve love's embrace
if love isn't on my each and every breath
it will not know my voice when I call
she told me no one falls in love
we are born with it all around us
not being in love
is no excuse for being out of it
that being said
you have work to do

withered

saw a
man
on the bus one morning
old worn t shirt
sweaty
withered ball cap
that gave up long before he did
old bag no handles
held tight to his chest
and saw a commentary on my life
I saw a 65 Chevy Nova
for sale

felt hope –
giving up
the purest sin

keep tempo baby
if you don't do nothing else
I told you
keep tempo

caught the attention
of a woman
staring directly
at my beard
smiling

as she made eye
contact with me
smiled as she continued
on her way
to destiny

destiny –
how the odds
flirt with you
sometimes

wanting something sweet
for no reason
the best reason
sometimes

when you see a woman smiling
a certain smile
you can almost hear
the dice rolling
such is life
such
is life
goes the roll
of the dice

estranged

tomorrow
is in love with me
has been for quite some time
but I'm in a relationship

estranged from today
still seeing yesterday
on the side –
tomorrow

knows I'm not happy
knows I may not be the victim
doesn't want what
I won't let go of

tomorrow
sees how I neglect
today
a day that wonders why

I don't just leave
sees the way I look at yesterday
wonders why I go back there
wonders if I ever really left

tomorrow
knows a lover:

will not let go of the past
can never hold your hand
knows a problem you don't want solved
is not the problem

will not have a lover
addicted to conflict
so she leaves me
to my maelstrom

tells me I only have what I want
says she can't be a party to my purgatory
but promises should I breakaway
when I am done

having such a ball
with my chains
she
will be waiting

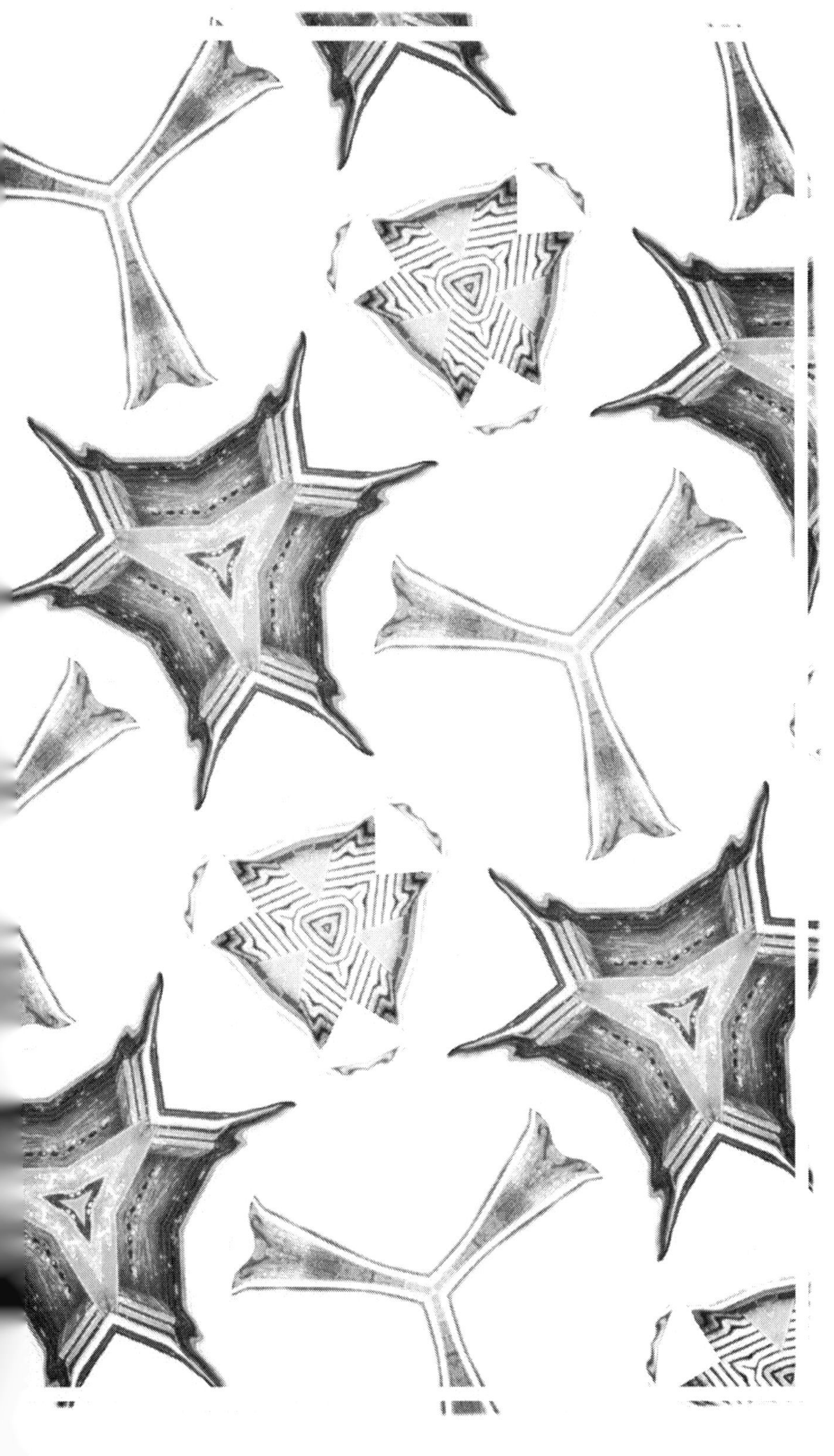

repeat

I will do my art
I will do the work
I will be the example
my existence
doesn't need
your permission

dear future lover (part two)

one day
we
will both
come home
quiet
and tired

we will eat
shower
put on clothes
that do not judge us
and watch Akira
as we fold
into each other

without speaking
we'll say
it's a good life

heaven

heaven will not be
a Las Vegas for the soul
St. Peter will not be the doorman
Mr. Wayne Newton
will not be performing
reminding everyone
he'll be there all week

there'll be no watered down
alcoholic beverages
compelling you to stay bound
to the blackjack tables
no cheap lobster dinners
or low priced buffets; because
no one eats in heaven

there will be no amusement parks
in heaven
no large, seemingly dangerous
yet thrilling, exciting ride
no one will have to wait in line for
just as you walk through the gates

there will be no fictional character
from your childhood waiting with a hat
balloon, or a drink cup shaped like him
her, or it; because
there are no lies in heaven

heaven will not be a huge field
where everyone is laughing
playing and frolicking; because
if you really wanted that
you would have done it
when you were here…on earth

there will be no huge glowing orb
unveiling all of life's mysteries to you
because knowing
won't matter; besides
instead of trying to solve
all of those questions; maybe
you should have tried living

the answer; you may see
familiar faces there; some
you'll be happy to see
some you won't even know
which isn't a problem; because
at that point names
do not matter; suffice to say
if you don't see anyone
you were expecting to see
there's no need to be surprised

there is no need
to regret not having said anything
more than you've already said; because
lament is an amenity

an earthly concern
it will not be a beautiful
living community
with homes available
before or after they are built
there will be no yard
you can make look better
than your neighbor's

none of the angels
will tend to the landscape; because
angels don't do that; unless
they're on earth
disguised as landscapers
which really only happens
in the movies

there will be no abundance
of anything you never had
no piles of it, none of it overflowing
waiting for you at long last
for the most part
whatever you've been waiting on
if you really needed it that bad
you'd already have it

you'd be where it is; on earth
as more than likely
it is not in heaven

there will be no streets
paved with gold
no fancy cars for you to drive in
no jewel-encrusted mansions
for each and every one; because
none of that matters
when you do not have
a corporeal body

you won't have to worry
about any one or any thing
anymore; there is no hate
in heaven

there will be no concierge
no room service, no one
to drive you around in a limo
no 3 to 4 shows in one night
no wax museums and St. Peter
will not be waiting
to open the gates
holding a plastic cup
full of coins for slot machines
only 144,000 will win anyway

heaven will not be
a Vegas
for the soul

hold

we are afraid
to release things
because losing the weight
only means ascension

the heights
scare us so much more
than the past
ever did

yesterday is your
co-dependent lover
and you are
emaciated

from the devotion
you are holding your
breath and it resents
you for it

there is a difference between
learning from your past and
being convinced by it
I don't know what path

you will choose but
I will tell you from experience
the easy way out
will only do you in

beseech

please bury your mustard
seed in my chest

I promise

I am fertile ground

the end of the day

in another life
I hope we'd be
married

maybe we'd be
butterflies

like the ones
left in my
stomach

funny how
time flies

when I'm trying
to reconcile
this unrest

in me, without
you; yet and still

why do fools
fall in love (a question)
well, maybe

we don't know
any better

since I've known

you, I haven't
known better

I tell myself
she got me
I've got to get her –
I left a message
after the beep

suggesting we
hookup

later on and maybe
baby, do more
than just creep

and maybe, baby
in our rhetoric

of seduction
you could check
your messages

and return my call
in the rusty afternoon

or in the moon-festooned
late night hours; your buttons
my voice, our atoms

message sent

by a friend

maybe, baby
then, I'd stop being
just a friend

this comic tragedy
could end; I could quit

wishing and waiting
closing my eyes
to see your face
I try to stay
an indelible man

around you; tough
with a soft spot
in the middle
yet and still, either way

waiting to be yours
by the end
of the day; waiting

for you to check
your messages

my message
waiting

victim of circumstance

I'm a penny with a hole in it
a man, a soul
shattered

life's a dog
her bark isn't half as bad
as her bite

despite her teeth
I fight; despite
my problems

I may just make it
if I try; it'd be a lie to say
I've no chance

my legs and feet still work
though they can't dance; as long
as they're strong enough

to make a stance
I'll always be more; more than
a victim of circumstance

stride

to the older cat
that had
a real
cool
walk
going
until he tripped
stumbled on that curve
somebody
obviously
put there
to mess up the groove
you had going

keep your stride, sir
I ain't seen shit

moon haiku

dear Moon; be it full
half or slim, I will always
long to kiss your face

I miss you

I find your absence
a nuisance; romance is an odd
unfathomable whale
without your presence

for every action a reaction
for every trek of light
track of my love
tracking your essence

anything less than
your essence, makes no sense
lost in this vortex
lost in a struggle

a chiaroscuro of you; light
and dark
when I start
and before I stop

an infinite uncertainty
and shadow
a withdrawal
without you

I desperately need a hit
of you; I am your arm
and you are my drug; time
has tied a strap around me

and the shadow
of the road ahead

has grabbed a needle full of you
and injected your light
your dark
inside me

I am an odd romance
when devoid of you
your touch, your smile
your eyes, capturing

all, with your stare
that we can't breath
the same air, that no one can do
what you do

that nothing fits the bill
that action
time, and space is a whale
of movement and

that my fate is a fixed star
to do nothing but wait
and fade, measured
in the err of time

molasses uphill
I truly believe

silence is the loudest
of all sounds; but
when I listen
I can hear

an S O S for you
time-capsule
a plea
making its way

through the space of action
and reaction, through light
and love through your essence
mine; a plea

for you to rescue me
we'd embrace; I'd say hello
with my eyes
rub the back of your neck

with one hand, and kiss you
despite all that's wrong
with us, our mixed up romance
is alright; and

despite all that is wrong
with us; no one
can do
what you do

surrogate

what I like is that I can feel good
around him; special; like I'm the one
I can do no wrong around him
I'm perfect; and it doesn't cost me a thing
I can cry to him laugh with him
hug him even get mad at him
as if he were the last guy
or the one I really want
and that is ok, because it's him

and I can do anything I want; it's as if
we're dating but not; or we're lovers
but not; it's as if we're married
but not; and that is okay; it's as if
I'm his girlfriend, only I'm a girl
and I'm his friend; and he accepts me
for who I am and who I'm not
even if I'm not his. I don't have to
hold his hand; I don't have to sit
next to him; I don't even have to
kiss him and we don't even have sex

well, we can have sex
but it's not like we have to
tell anybody, because we're not really
like that; because it's him

all he'll do is smile and rationalize us
he does a lot of that

which really helps
because I need to feel good
about who I am; what we are
because we are not really like that
I mean, I might even get
a real boyfriend one day
but why hurry?

I mean, he's everything
I could want in a man
I don't want; but
I might actually like him
I'd even consider being
what he needs if he
didn't make it so damn easy for me
if he didn't make excuses

all the time; it's like he is scared
to be alone; he'll accept anything
from anyone willing to stay
he makes the cutest recycling bin
and, I'm a firm believer
in recycling; I think he has issues
of some kind; he has walls
I've no time to climb
because honestly

that is his deal and shit
I just want a damn hug

love

love says *don't*

love says
hold your best friend's hand
and it will make up
for each day
someone said

I love you

without meaning it.
love says *do not try*
to make this poem something
people will like; it says I will hold
your hand even
if I don't know you

love says *even though*
you are not my blood
you are worth spilling for

love says
I make no promises
but have strong
aspirations and
I need you to see
I'm trying.

love says

you gotta start somewhere
but trying ain't enough
you deserve better
than words made
of glass

love
is not brick shaped syllables
or thoughts
you could have
crafted better

love understands
it is the strength
pain left behind
it does not leave you; it says
I only confuse you
when you do not pay
attention; love
is sometimes found
in your junk mail

love is not the peak
you dread, but the peak
to be surmounted

love says *you will find me*
in the heaven of endurance

love says *speak up*
we can't hear you

love says *you deserve*
to be loved for who you are

love costs and there will be
lots of change; and it ain't trickin
if you got it; it works in progress
therefore if you work at it
there will be progress

love is not a metaphor
for anything else
you're just putting too much
thought into it

love means you're more than
a secret; do not romanticize
being someone's secret

love says *you are more than*
the sum of your likes; it is the challenge
you rise to. It is humbling

love says *there is a reason*
its name has been repeated
throughout this poem

love says *there is no meme*
abbreviation, or cute misspelling
good enough to say if it's real

it says *laugh at something*

or with someone; it is like post-defecation
euphoria, because it feels so good
after all this time
to just let shit go

it says *this would not*
have been a poem
about love if it didn't
mention dancing

love requires the sacrifice
of ego; the offering
of your discomfort; that
you struggle; that you give into
its uncertainty; that you accept
you are an odd romance; you are
like the light traveling
between us all; all of us
stardust; alive and breathing

like love, and this poem
could go on, but these words
are not the heart of affection
these words are only a poem
and that which defines love
hopes you do more
than read about it

green bow

you could tear your house down
reduce it to bits
if you had the strength
to walk out of it

even then, it would not
be worth it to do so; to chance
leaving splinters of the past
in your heart

I confess I've never had to tear
my dwelling down; its hate is mine
its love, mine; we breathe the same air
cannot help but give

one another life; to remind
each other of our need for shelter
I suppose it's still there, I suppose
I could build you a new one

if it wasn't; if you wanted
I'd clear it out; you could live
in any room you wish; don't mind
the pieces of paper

don't read them
little things

I've noted about you

I don't want you to read them

I am dumb enough to know
what this is; I have the gumption
the patience to wait for you
in the forest

should you see me
past the trees

know my hands are
big and
wide and
ample

I could catch you
if you were to fall
I could shelter you
if you were to tear

your house down
you'd lay there; in the valley
of my palms

we'd grow stronger, together
we'd take in the days
we are still here; we are
our own reward

I would
every day

mouth
shut

wait
for you
Jenny

I would not feel this way
were I not tethered to you

you tell me to run
in the end I will

where
is up to you
Jenny.

you are not mine, you
are your own hero

I am
just a
big dumb
GRIN

hands and arms
spread open; a shelter
past the trees; if
you needed one

skirmish

love is war; only
because we would rather fight
it, than fight for it

hardy ivy park

you won't read this
but for a brief moment
I missed you; thought
about
you
down
in my
soul

sat in the park
and remembered the last
time I let your eyes
take hold of me
while you rubbed
the back of my head
your slight
of hand; your open-palm
letters; you were like
a salve of light
unto my heart

you won't see this
because
we can't even be
friends now; our minds
taut; filled with
intolerance; but
for a moment
I remembered

the last time
it was quiet here
I remembered
the last
time
love
was
a noun

conscious

like I knew
what I was doing
I said it, but
it was hopeless
to apologize

what bewildered
me was after a while
she just got quiet
which means
she won

my willingness
to atone; music
to her ears; happy
feelings
in the air

I love the music
we make; without her
I am a one hit
wonder; a mixed-up
tape; I wonder

why she hadn't
shown up sooner

us

I couldn't say what I wanted to
the air was thick
I wanted to speak
every discernable word
the two or three hundred
between my teeth
desperately seeking refuge
behind my lips, but
now the air between us
is nowhere near as thin
as it used to be; we are strangers
held captive by our words
or vice versa because
we won't let them escape

we have both fallen captive
to the seduction of egocentricity
the stillness; reputation; the strain
of disposition; and the tension
in the oxygen has left us mistresses
much less than friends
now there's no longer a permanence
between us; when it comes to you
and me there is no longer *we*
to discuss and now we talk
about you and I
to everyone else, but us

bones

my soul holds
these bones
for you; these bones
set upon this stone
in days that revel the possibility
of time travel; in a mindful hell
taxed by flesh and blood
taxed in the tragedy
our calamity of not being god-like
immortal as the genus of iris or the azaleas
in this Earth's soil, Sun's light
you have long since given up
dreaming of the blossoming
of your bosom
dreaming of immortality
dreaming that we had
the time of Gods
now it has been so long
even the sea sits still
even my flesh has left me
but my soul holds
these bones hold
no infinitesimal measure
of stardust

heaven and hell will be too long
I will stay upon my stone
practice my smile
for when I see you again

haiku 5

bare no envy or
ill will; hate costs, love is free
and shit, I got bills

aesthetic

visualizing
the very shape
of her thighs
inch by inch

as you
simultaneously
caress warm curves
she giggles

one
because you're staring her directly in the eyes
post coitus
and

two
her booty is mad ticklish
the goose bumps only confirm as they read
like braille –
thank you

applesauce

she will be what she is
a beautiful girl
sepia skin; kissed
by the sun

she was born
her very own
shade of brown
hue of wisdom

in the corners; cute nose
angel's ears; with a smile
vaccinating her laughter
inoculates you

she will crayon color within the lines
she will etch beyond barriers,
closing her eyes.

she has a thing for applesauce

there will be days
where applesauce
will be the only thing
that stands between us
and total annihilation.

there are things she will find out on her own
at some point, she will want to fly

she will win altitude for believing she had
a place in the clouds

she'll befriend logic and love
her dreams no less; she will avoid
going crazy by not fighting it
dancing where she pleases
twirling, swaying and jumping
in the air and the rain and the void
as if this place were
the only worthy place

she'll have the right to remain silent
though it will never be a precedent
while she may never tell you everything
she won't need to; she'll speak her mind
not her mouth; she'll have the right
to be a problem; treasure rebirth
as the solution; loving her
won't be easy, but can help
if respecting her is difficult; one day
she'll find a woman in the mirror
they'll love each other forever
her real beauty will be found
in strength, sacrifice, and resilience
even the dreams she doesn't want
will guide her; but sometimes
she'll stop; rest her hands at her backside
she will breathe; and
she'll keep going

that is what heroes do

you're a hero

you will always believe
in magic, but there will be days
where you will speak
incantations like – *daddy*
you will look
for the first man
to ever love you
with a space for him
in your heart shaped
like the vacant seat
at your tea parties
I won't be there

on the days you need help
touching at the sky
I won't be there

lost butterfly kisses
wishes from birthdays
nonrefundable –
daddy how do I look
I won't be there; and you
will still look for me

within the crevices
of your memory

saving me a space
in possibility; all the same
with or without my love
you'll keep moving

this is what you will do

you will write the pages
of your own destiny
while living in the key
of your own song

at the end of your day
there will be a place
outside, where the sun
can't wait to play with you
and the wind and rain
can't wait to dance
with you

there will be
laughter; and tears

and applesauce

you will be
what you already
are; and that is
just the beginning

74 till infinity

I am a half empty notebook

metronome churches
dead tree containers

I am too many pockets

empty house haunted
by a black boy's ghost

I am a room full of prayers
hugging life

benevolence bursting
from blood vessels

that which does not kill me is very persistent
at trying

that which does not kill
me, is poetry; is cunning

I am afraid one day God will finish writing
me

I am a pawnshop-heart one step from selling
to a stranger's eyes

any day now
any day now

I am hoping to die asleep
and finished
in the comfort
of my home

rather than bustling
rather than shuddered

I am a home
wherever I stand
a castle to some; fortified
protons and neutrons

and idiosyncrasies

here and gone
at the same time

I am a half empty notebook

with pages
left

ABOUT THE AUTHOR

Joe Brundidge is an author, host, and public speaker living in Austin, Texas. He has hosted a number of open mics for almost 20 years to include his own show, *Spoken & Heard* at Kick Butt Coffee. He also served as the Director of the Austin International Poetry Festival for three years, from 2012-2015.

Made in the USA
Columbia, SC
17 May 2019